AF594694

16 Pictures Robert Grosvenor

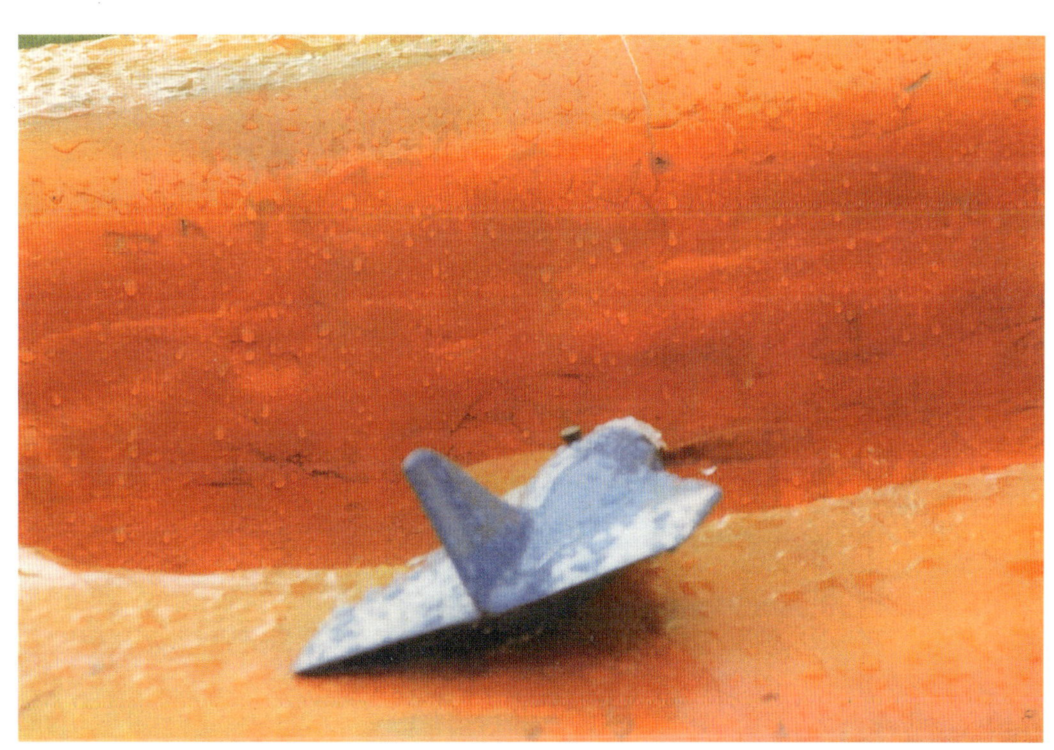

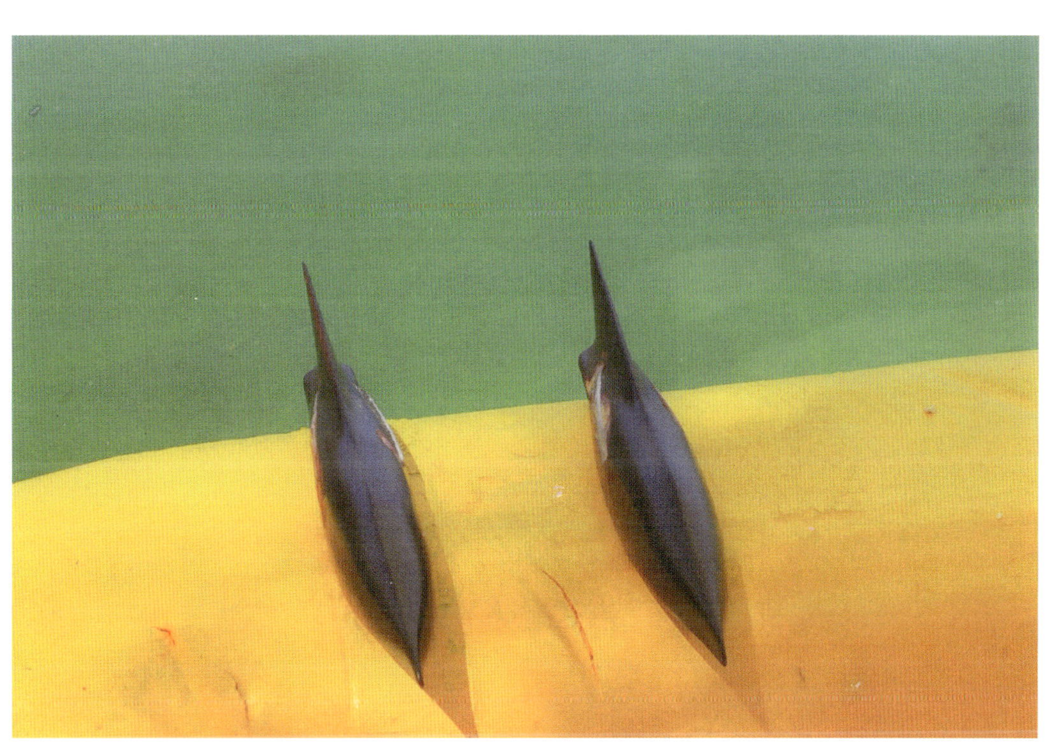

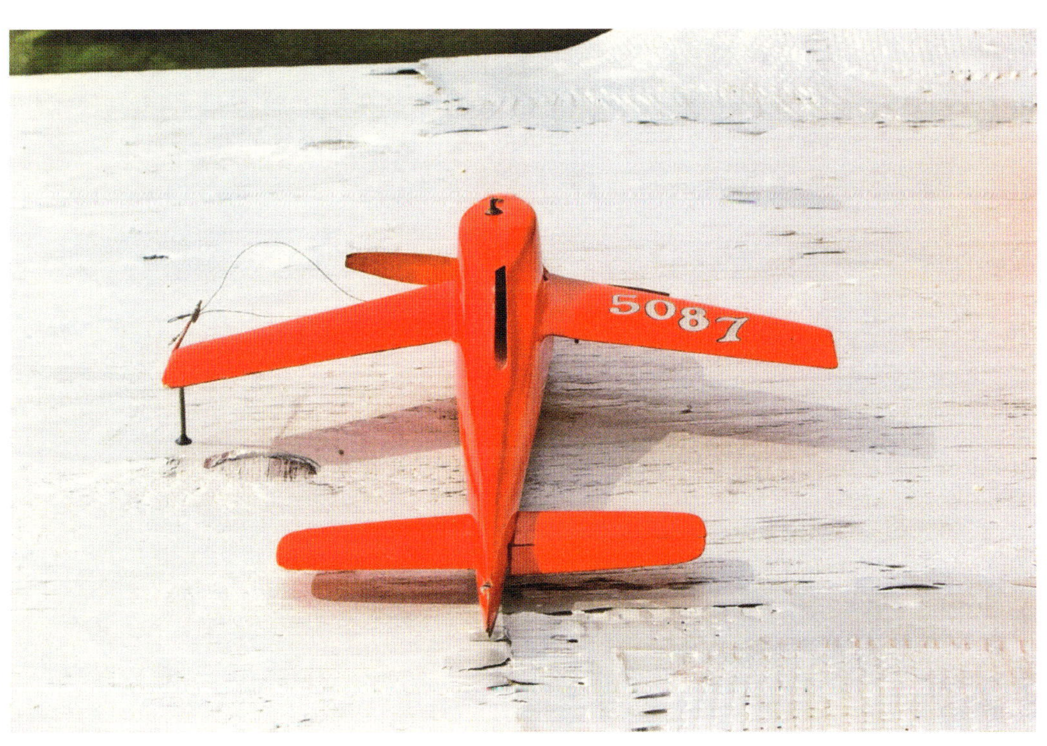
5087

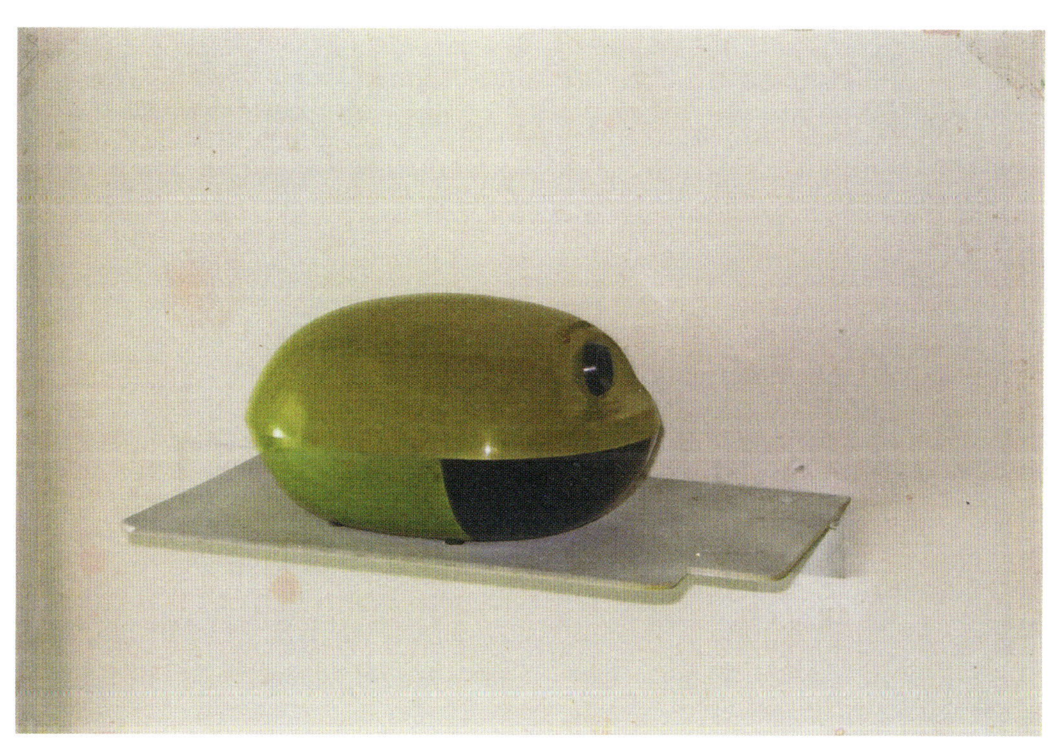

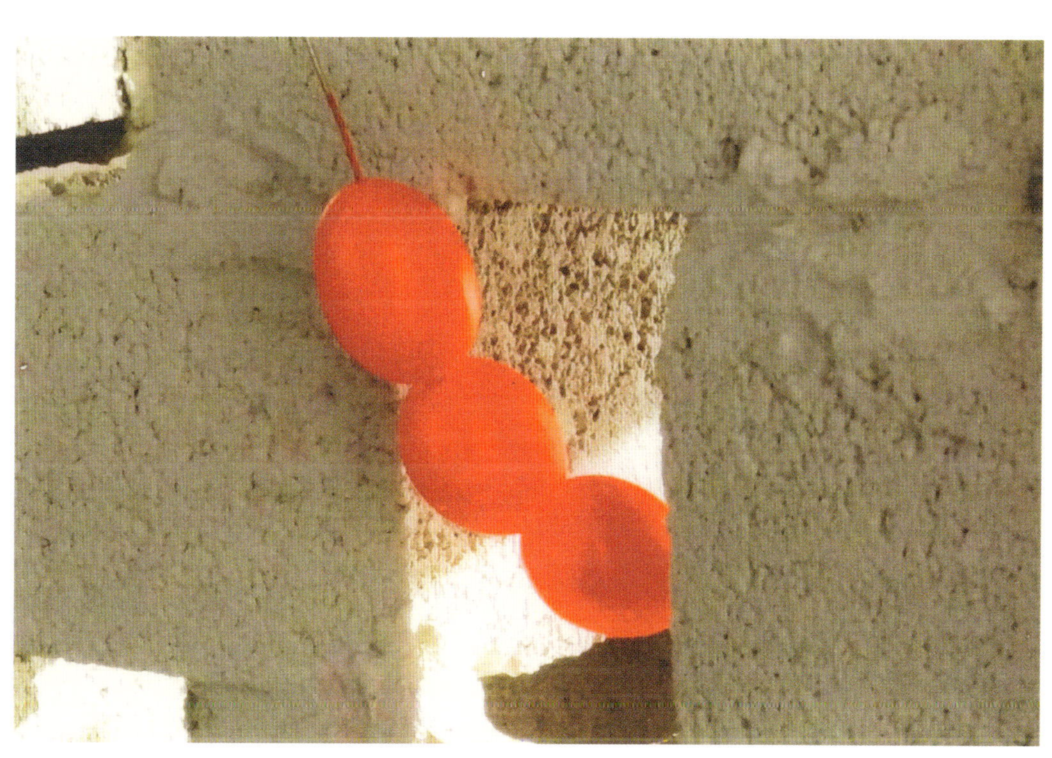

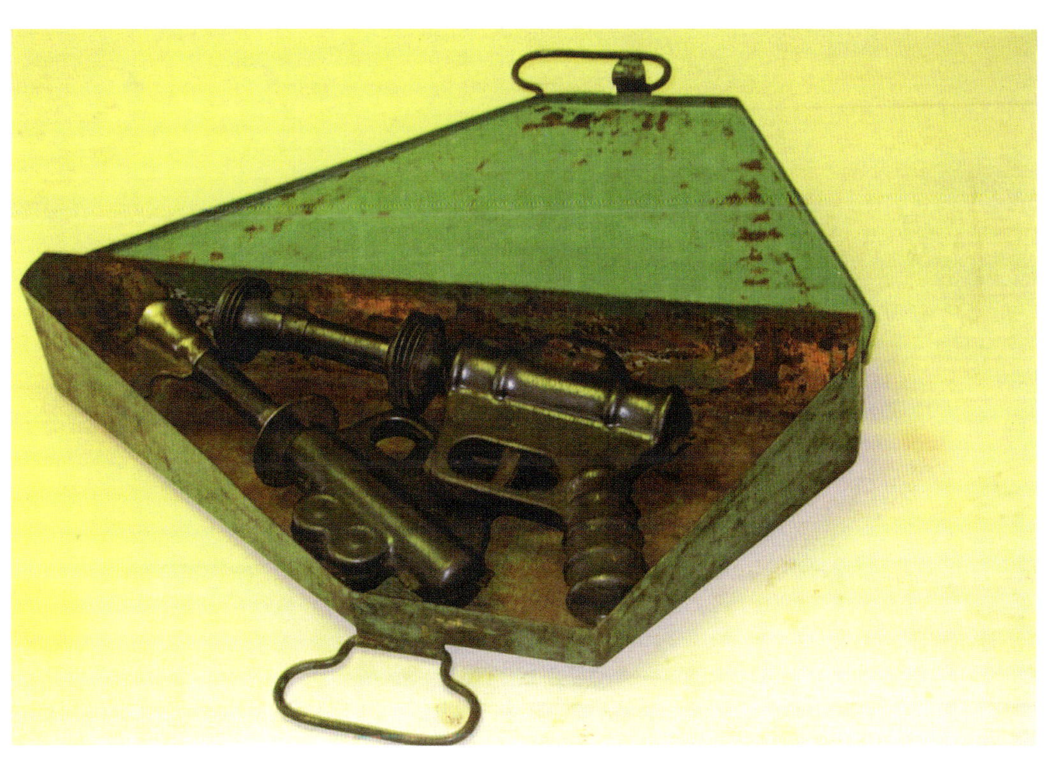

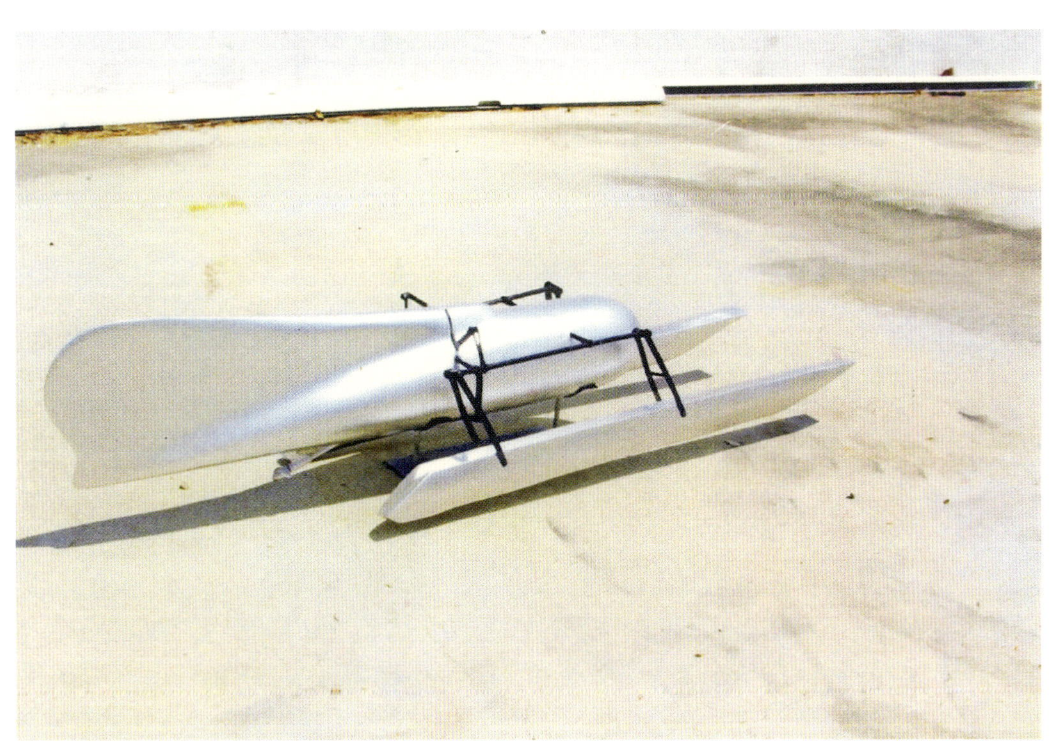

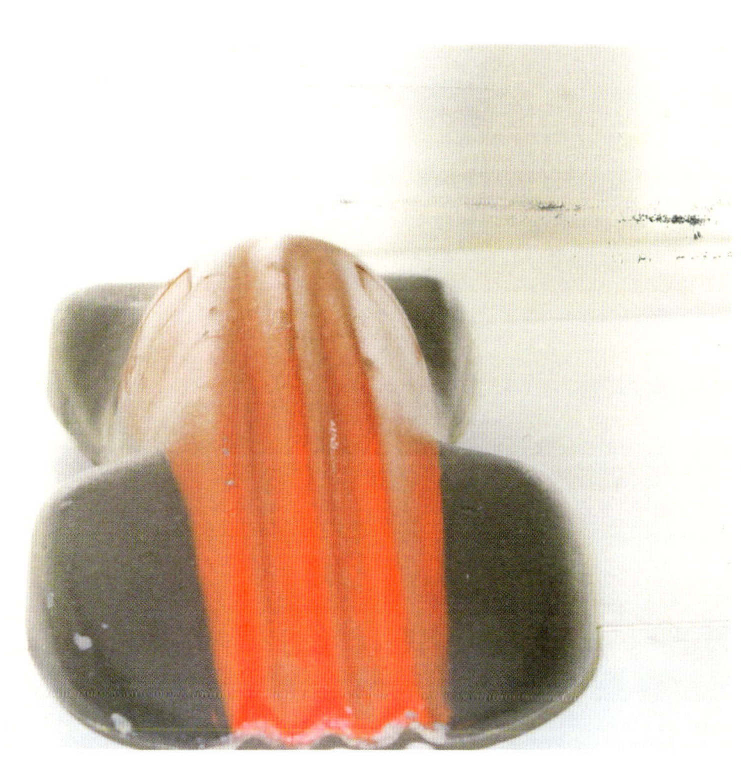

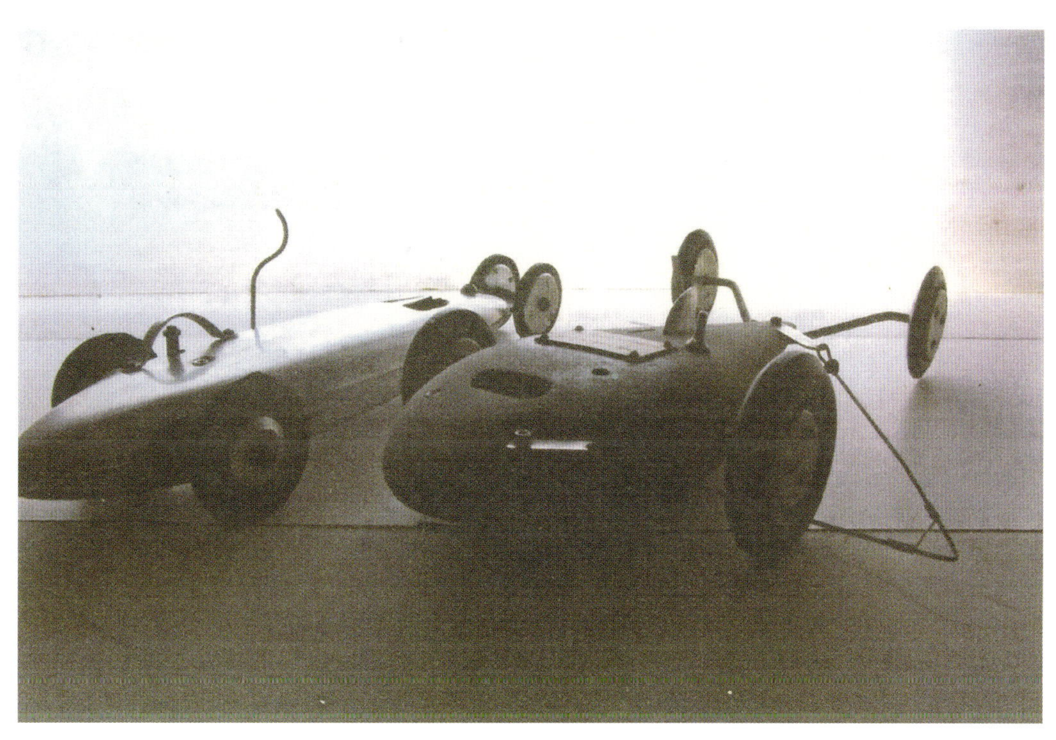

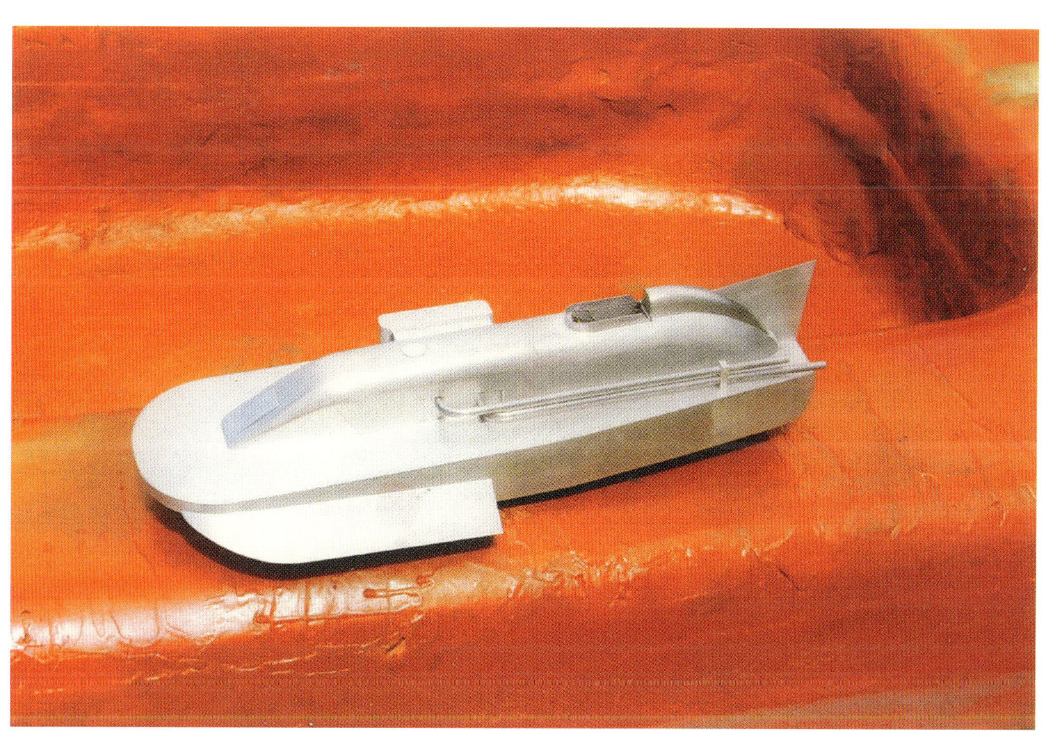

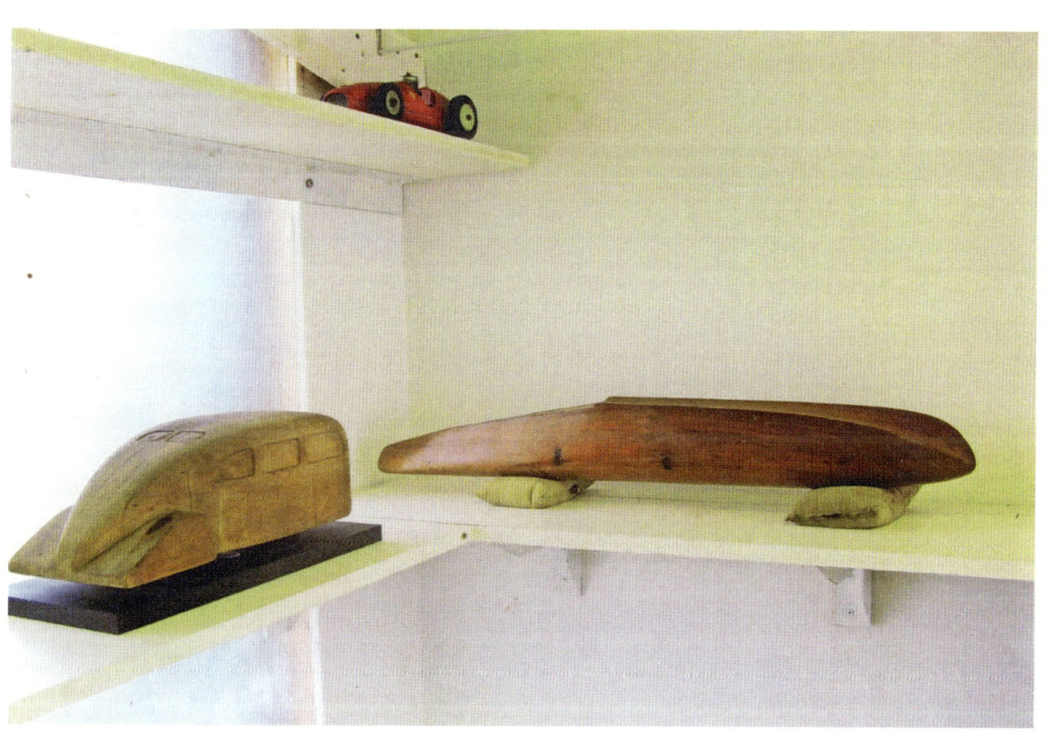

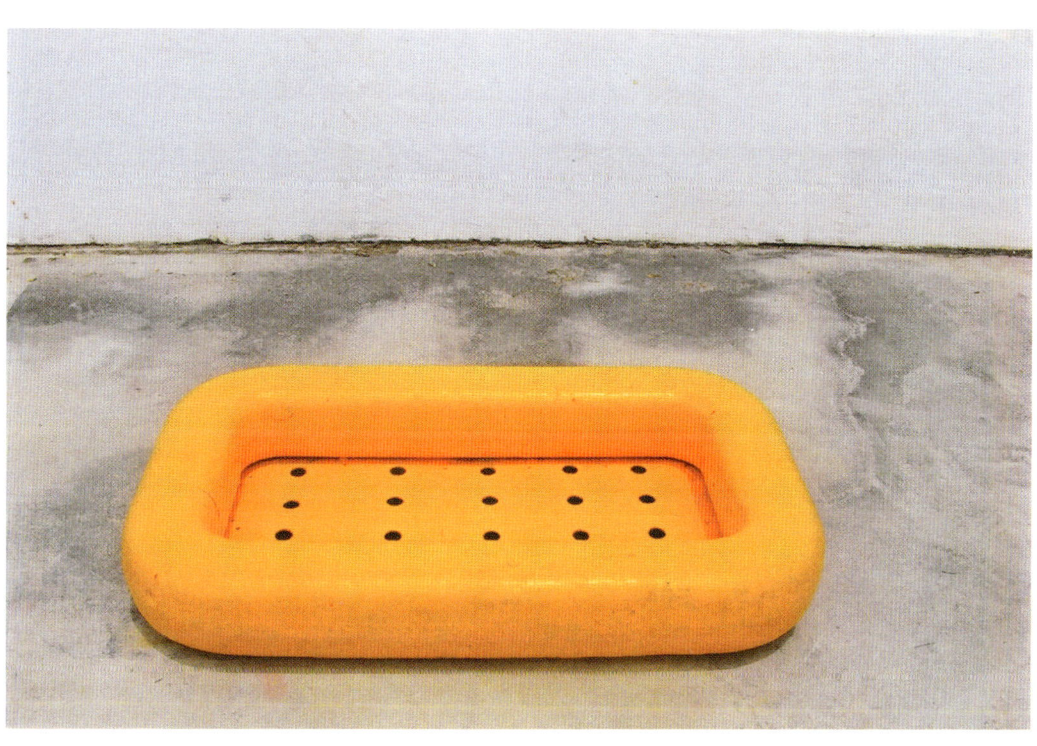

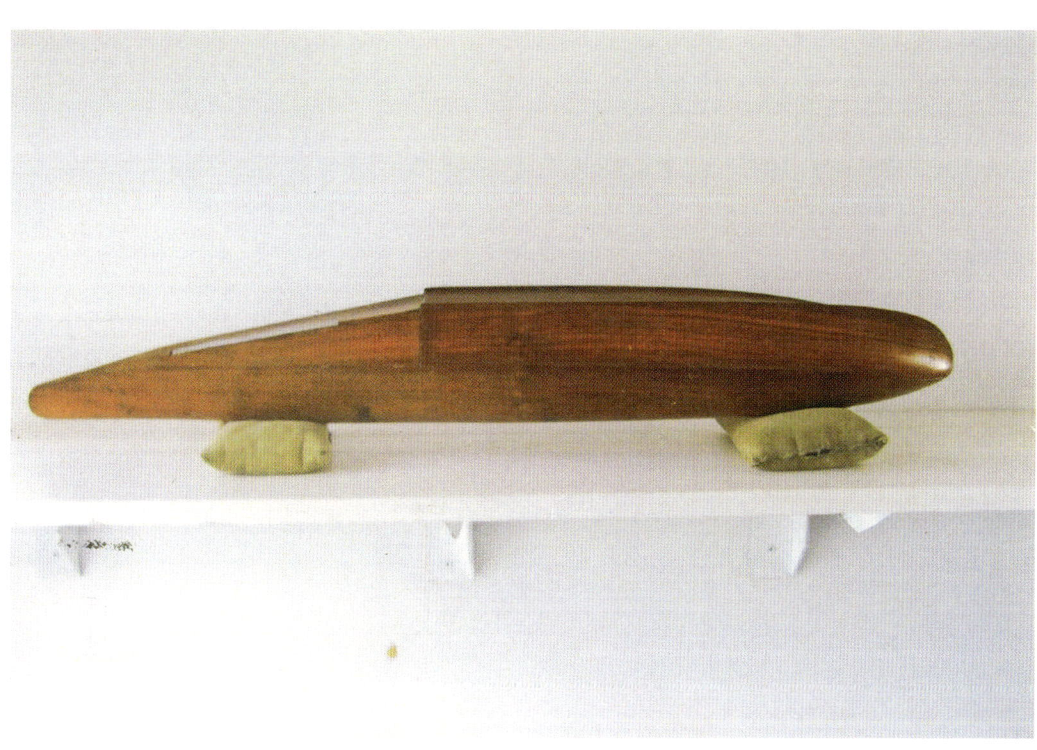

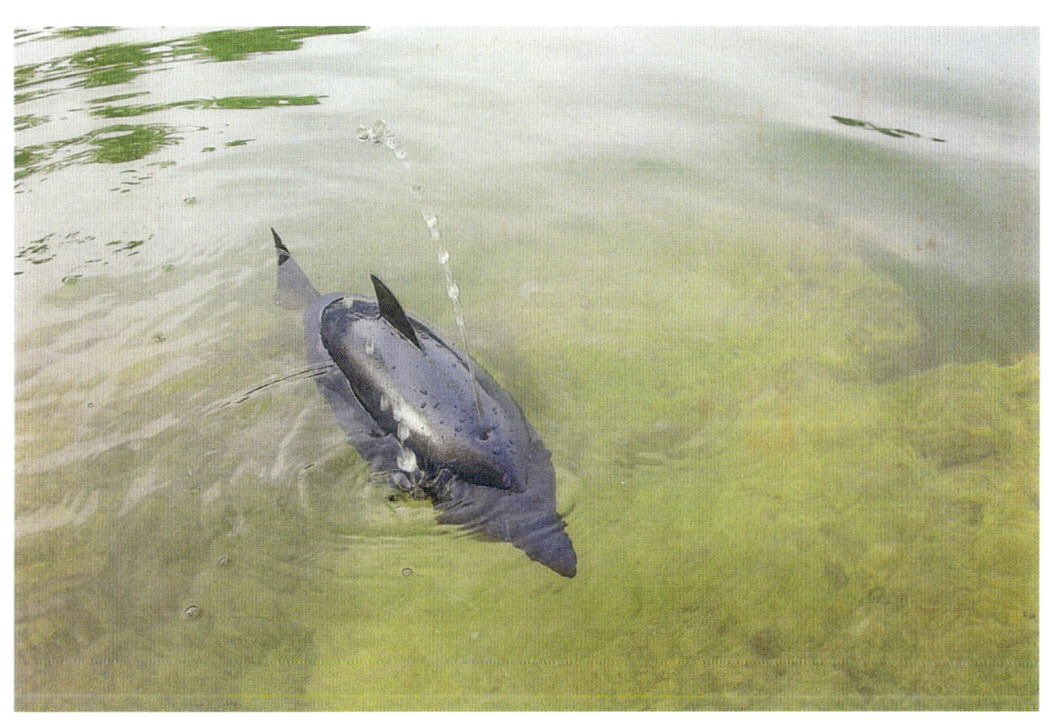

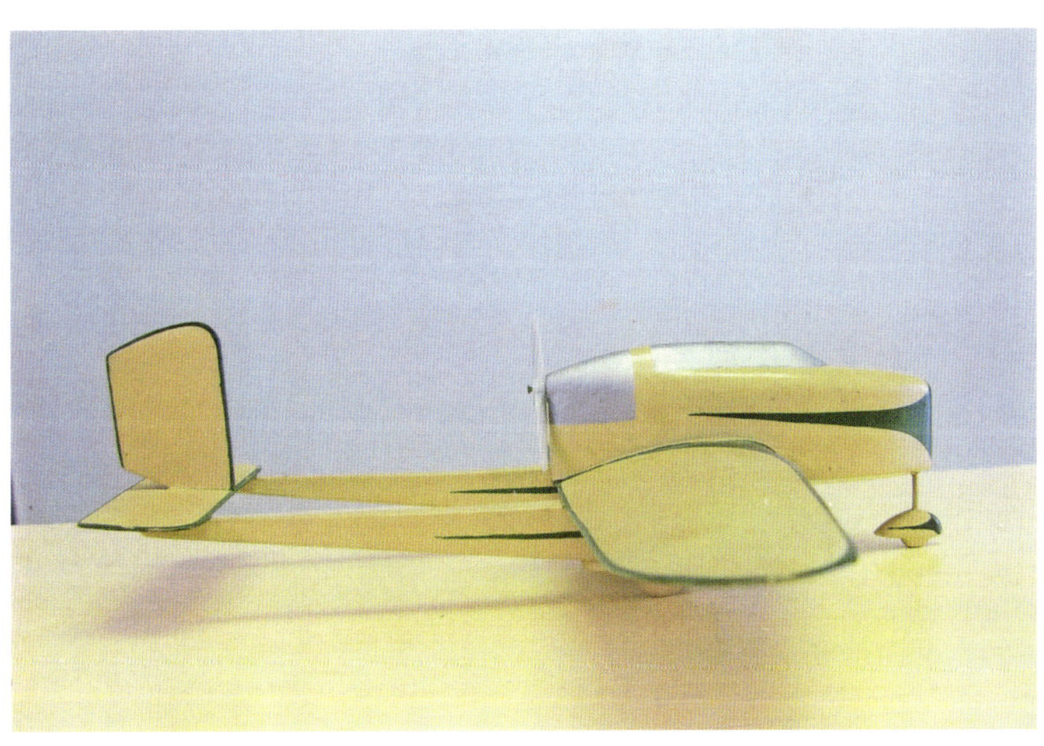

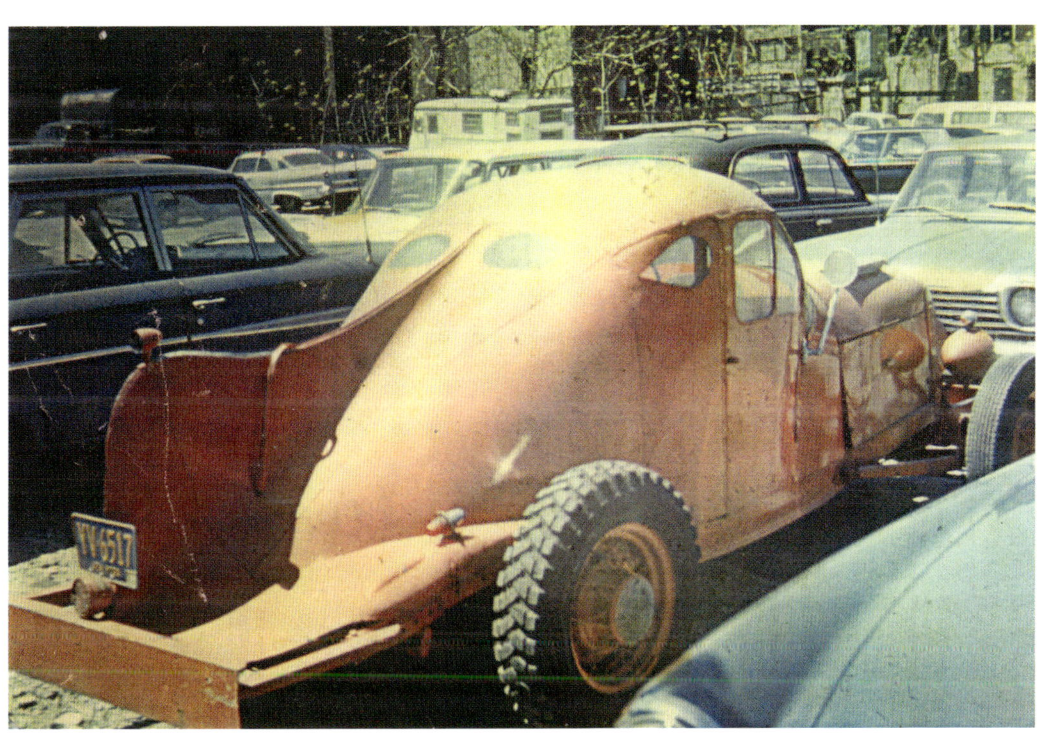

Robert Grosvenor
16 Pictures

Published by Karma, New York
Edition of 750
ISBN 978-1-942607-74-8

Special thanks to Paula Cooper Gallery.